Digital Detox: Bloom Beyond the Noise

How to Heal from Notification Overload, Reclaim Your Focus

Abby Nagra

Digital Detox: Bloom Beyond The Noise : How To Heal From Notification Overload, Reclaim Your Focus
by **Abby Nagra**

Published with **BookFylo**
Noida, Delhi NCR, India
www.bookfylo.com
support@bookfylo.com

ISBN and barcode are on the back cover.
Printed & distributed using print-on-demand technology.

Preface

We live in a time where our minds rarely rest.

Every buzz, every scroll, every tiny red dot pulls at our attention, fragmenting our thoughts and sometimes, our sense of self.

This book was born from that quiet exhaustion, the kind that comes not from doing too much but from being constantly switched on.

I began to notice how easy it was to reach for my phone instead of my thoughts, to check in with screens before checking in with my heart.

It made me wonder when rest began to feel like rebellion.

Digital Detox is not about abandoning technology or disconnecting from the world.

It is about learning to live with it differently, consciously, kindly, and without losing yourself in the process.

It is about reclaiming your mornings before the glow of a screen, about rediscovering real conversations that do not need filters, and about finding stillness in moments that do not need to be shared.

Through these pages, I hope to remind you that peace is not something we find online.

It is something we cultivate quietly, in the space between one breath and the next.

This is not a manual. It is a mirror.

A reflection of what happens when you choose presence over pressure, meaning over noise, and yourself above all.

May you find calm where there once was chaos, and rediscover the beauty of living unplugged yet fully alive.

Abby Nagra

About the author

Abby Nagra believes in the quiet strength of slowing down and the beauty of reconnecting with oneself in a world that moves too fast. Digital Detox: Bloom Beyond the Noise is her first published book and a deeply personal reflection on finding calm, clarity, and balance amid modern distractions.

Through her writing, Abby gently encourages readers to rediscover stillness, nurture mindful habits, and create small moments of peace and presence in their everyday lives.

Beyond writing, she finds joy in quiet walks, journaling, and embracing the simple moments that make life feel meaningful and alive.

Table of Contents

Introduction: The Overstimulated Mind

We wake up and scroll before we even remember our dreams. Mornings often begin with headlines, messages, and endless updates, all before we even greet ourselves. The modern world has replaced silence with constant scrolling. Every ping, every red dot, and every notification gives our brain a small hit of dopamine. That instant spark of validation is addictive, and over time, this overstimulation rewires how we think, feel, and connect.

Your nervous system is constantly "on call" without you even noticing. Every message that goes unanswered, every unread badge, and every news story builds tiny layers of stress known as micro-stress. Those layers accumulate, making you anxious when you are offline, restless when you are still, and disconnected even when surrounded by people.

This is not about blaming technology. It is about reclaiming balance. You deserve to live a life in which your peace is not interrupted by notifications.

Chapter 1: The Myth of Connection

We live in a world that tells us we are never truly alone. Notifications, messages, likes, and comments create an illusion of constant interaction. On the surface, it feels like connection, but often, it is something much less.

True connection is about presence. It is about feeling seen, heard, and understood. Yet, so often, our digital lives give us the opposite. We scroll endlessly, chasing interactions that leave us emptier than before. A heart-stopping notification can feel like joy, but once it fades, the quiet loneliness remains.

We convince ourselves that being online, sharing pictures, updating statuses, and reacting to every story keeps us close to people. But do we ever stop to notice how we feel in those moments? Do we ask ourselves if we are really connecting or simply consuming a filtered version of life?

There is a subtle difference between being present and being available. Availability is easy. It is instantaneous. Presence is deeper. Presence requires intention, focus, and a willingness to engage without distraction. The more we confuse availability with presence, the more we fall into the trap of digital overstimulation.

Many of us live parallel lives like one online, one offline. We post images of joy while feeling disconnected internally. We send messages that express connection, yet inside, we feel isolated. Our minds are fragmented, constantly pinging between what is happening in reality and what is happening on our screens.

Consider this: how often have you been in the same room with someone, yet both of you were scrolling on your phones instead of talking? Or found yourself laughing at a meme while feeling a quiet, nagging emptiness inside? These small, daily moments are subtle reminders that our version of connection is often shallow, fleeting, and incomplete.

The myth of connection is seductive because it promises closeness without effort. It whispers that if we keep scrolling, liking, posting, and messaging, we will feel whole. But wholeness is not found in pixels or notifications. It is found in the moments where we look up from our screens, take a deep breath, and engage with life as it actually exists.

Digital tools are not the problem. They are the medium. The real challenge lies in how we interact with them. Without intention, our attention is stolen, our energy drained, and our sense of self diluted. The more we allow our time online to dominate, the more we forget what it feels like to be truly present within ourselves and with others.

Breaking free from this myth begins with awareness. Notice the patterns in your digital life. Ask yourself: when did I last feel fully present in a conversation without checking my phone? When did I last look at the sky, listen to the wind, or savor a moment without documenting it for an audience?

Awareness is the first step toward reclaiming control and rediscovering the depth of real connection.

It also requires courage. It is not easy to step back from habits that have become automatic, comforting, and socially validated. There will be moments of discomfort when you unplug, when silence replaces the constant chatter of notifications. But these are the moments where growth begins.

Imagine sitting with a friend without a phone between you, or enjoying a quiet morning without reaching for a screen. Imagine the depth of presence when your attention is undivided, and your mind is fully there. This is not nostalgia. It is a choice. A choice to prioritize meaningful connection over constant availability, authenticity over performance, and presence over noise.

Connection is not measured in likes, comments, or followers. It is measured in depth, attention, and authenticity. It is measured in moments of real laughter, tears shared, and attention given without distraction. And the first step toward true connection begins with you, with awareness, and with the courage to unplug long enough to remember what it feels like to be fully alive.

Reflection Exercises:

- Take a moment today to notice how many times you reach for your phone in an hour. Pause and ask yourself what you are truly seeking with each check. Is it connection, distraction, or simply habit? Write down three ways you can reconnect with yourself or someone close to you without your device.

- Observe your surroundings for five minutes without a phone. What do you see, hear, or feel? Note the details and sensations you normally miss.

Chapter 2: The Attention Economy and Your Energy

We live in a world where our attention has become a commodity. Every notification, alert, and ping is designed to capture it, pulling you into an invisible economy where your focus is the most valuable currency. Companies, apps, and platforms compete relentlessly for this currency, and often, you are the one paying the cost not in money, but in energy, clarity, and peace of mind.

Even small interactions like scrolling through social media, checking emails, responding to messages often take more energy than you realize. Each split second of divided attention requires your brain to constantly shift gears, a process psychologists call “task-switching.” It may feel effortless, but over time, it depletes your mental and emotional reserves. Multitasking feels productive, yet it leaves your mind tired, scattered, and less capable of deep focus.

Have you ever noticed how your energy dips after scrolling for just ten minutes? Or how a simple task like writing an email feels exhausting after hours online? This is subtle fatigue, but it is real. It affects your creativity, your emotional resilience, and even your ability to enjoy the present moment. Attention without intention consumes your energy without offering meaningful returns.

The attention economy also thrives on comparison. Social media, news feeds, and online communities constantly show curated versions of life. The happiest moments, the biggest successes, the most exciting adventures are all condensed into snapshots. When we scroll, we unconsciously measure our lives against these highlights. The result is often dissatisfaction, restlessness, or self-doubt. This invisible form of exhaustion drains energy silently, leaving you feeling less than, even when everything appears fine on the surface.

Even leisure time can be misleading. Hours spent browsing, watching videos, or flipping between apps can feel relaxing, but too often they leave you mentally foggy and emotionally flat. True restoration comes not from passive consumption, but from intentional engagement like quiet reflection, mindful walks, or meaningful conversations.

The cost of attention is not always obvious. You might feel "busy" without producing anything meaningful. You might feel connected while feeling lonely. You might be constantly "on" while forgetting how to rest. Every interaction online has a subtle impact on your energy, whether you notice it or not.

Understanding this connection between attention and energy is the first step toward reclaiming both. When we realize that every digital interaction consumes a piece of our focus, we can start to make intentional choices. We can set boundaries, create mindful habits, and invest our energy in what truly matters.

Reflection Exercises:

- Track how much time you spend online in a day. Note which activities energize you and which leave you drained. Reflect on why certain interactions feel fulfilling while others feel empty.
- Choose one common digital habit that consumes your energy. Commit to adjusting it perhaps limiting social media use, checking emails only twice a day, or taking short screen breaks. Observe how this change affects your mental clarity, mood, and energy levels.
- Real-life stories illustrate this clearly. Think of a friend who scrolls for hours in the evening and then complains about being exhausted the next day. Or consider your own experience: a morning that starts with phone checking and ends with fatigue before lunch. These are not isolated experiences; they are symptoms of an attention economy designed to fragment focus and capture energy.

Breaking free does not mean rejecting technology. It means engaging with it consciously. It means choosing when to be online, what to focus on, and what deserves your undivided attention. By protecting your attention, you protect your energy the very resource that allows you to feel alive, present, and capable.

Reflection Exercise:

- At the end of your day, write down three moments when you felt fully present without screens, notifications, or distractions. Consider how these moments affected your mood, energy, and sense of connection.

Energy and attention are intertwined. When one is drained, the other suffers. By reclaiming attention, you reclaim vitality. By reclaiming focus, you reclaim your life. And this chapter is the first step toward understanding how to do just that, so you can move forward into the rest of this book with intention, awareness, and a renewed sense of calm.

Chapter 3: The Emotional Detox

Just as our bodies need cleansing, our minds and hearts require detoxification. We carry invisible weight like the subtle stress, anxiety, comparison, and digital overload that accumulate day by day. This is not always obvious. You may feel "fine," yet underneath, tension quietly chips away at your energy, patience, and clarity.

The first step in an emotional detox is awareness. Notice what you are carrying. Is it worry about missed messages, anxiety from social media updates, or lingering tension from interactions online? These small, constant stressors build up, like invisible clutter in your mind. Over time, they affect how you feel, think, and respond to the world.

Emotional detox is about intentionally releasing this weight. It is about creating space for calm, clarity, and balance. It starts with a pause like stepping away from the noise, observing your feelings without judgment, and allowing yourself to breathe fully. This is not avoidance; it is conscious care.

Consider how often your emotions are triggered by screens and notifications. A comment, a news alert, or a story can provoke frustration, sadness, or envy. These emotions are valid, yet they are amplified by constant exposure. The emotional detox teaches you to notice, process, and release rather than absorb and carry them.

Real-life example: imagine finishing a long day of scrolling through feeds and reading headlines. You might feel exhausted, anxious, or irritated, even if nothing "bad" happened. This is emotional residue of subtle stress that accumulates unnoticed. The detox is the process of recognizing it and gently letting it go.

A key part of this process is reflection. Journaling, mindful observation, and breathing exercises help you acknowledge your emotional state without becoming overwhelmed. For instance, take five minutes to write down what thoughts or feelings are taking up your mental space. Once observed, ask yourself: do these thoughts deserve my attention? Can I release them for now and focus on what nourishes me?

Another important step is setting boundaries. Emotional detox is not only internal; it is also external. Limit interactions that drain your energy, curate the digital content you consume, and be selective about where you invest your attention. Protecting your emotional space is essential for clarity and well-being.

Reflection Exercises:

- At the end of each day, write down three emotional "weights" you experienced. Identify whether they were influenced by digital interactions, external stressors, or internal pressures. Then, consciously release them with a deep breath or a small ritual perhaps a short walk, meditation, or journaling.

- Create a “digital calm window” in your day such as period of at least 30 minutes when you are completely offline. Observe how your mood, focus, and emotional state shift during this time. Record your observations.

The emotional detox is also about rewiring your responses. Instead of automatically reacting to notifications, news, or online drama, you learn to pause, observe, and choose your response. This conscious awareness reduces emotional fatigue and increases resilience.

Finally, emotional detox is about reconnection with yourself. By releasing what no longer serves you, you make room for clarity, creativity, and presence. You begin to notice the small joys that are often drowned out by digital noise: the sound of birds, a quiet conversation, a moment of reflection, or the satisfaction of completing a task without distraction.

Your energy and emotions are intimately linked. By detoxing emotionally, you restore your vitality, focus, and inner peace. This chapter is the bridge from understanding the drain caused by the attention economy to creating practical ways to reclaim your energy and live intentionally.

Chapter 4: The Art of Slowing Down

In a world that glorifies speed, slowing down feels almost rebellious. We are taught to measure life by how much we accomplish, how quickly we respond, and how many goals we chase. Yet the more we hurry, the further we drift from presence, peace, and meaning.

The art of slowing down is not about doing less. It is about doing things with awareness. It is about creating space between moments instead of racing through them. It is learning to move with intention rather than momentum.

When we slow down, we begin to notice the texture of life. The warmth of sunlight on the skin, the rhythm of your breath, the soft hum of the world when it is quiet. These moments remind us that life is not a checklist; it is a series of experiences to be felt fully.

At first, slowing down can feel uncomfortable. The silence feels strange, the stillness brings restlessness. We are so used to stimulation that calm feels unfamiliar. Yet this discomfort is a sign of healing. Your mind and body are adjusting to a gentler rhythm after years of constant motion.

Slowing down does not mean giving up your responsibilities or ambitions. It means honoring your own pace. It means understanding that rest is not a reward you earn after exhaustion but a right that allows you to live more fully.

Imagine a morning where you begin your day without checking your phone. You take a few deep breaths, stretch, and sip your tea or coffee slowly. You notice the quiet around you. In that moment, nothing has changed outside, yet inside you feel lighter, more grounded, and more human. That is the quiet power of slowing down.

Modern life rewards urgency. Fast replies, quick results, and constant visibility have become normal. But presence cannot be rushed. True creativity, love, and clarity grow in the stillness that slowing down provides.

The art of slowing down also extends to how we consume information, make decisions, and connect with others. Try pausing before responding to a message. Take a breath before reacting to news. Eat your meal without distractions. Each pause is a small act of awareness that gently brings you back to yourself.

Slowing down reconnects you with your intuition. In stillness, your inner voice becomes clearer. You begin to sense what feels right for you, what drains you, and what nourishes you. When life becomes quieter, your wisdom rises naturally.

Reflection Exercises:

- Think of three areas in your daily routine where you can consciously slow down. This could be your morning ritual, eating meals, or winding down before sleep.

Practice presence during these times and notice how it changes your mood and energy.

- Set aside ten minutes each day for stillness. No screens, no distractions, no agenda. Simply sit, breathe, and observe. At first your mind may wander, and that is normal. The more you practice, the more natural stillness becomes.

Slowing down also deepens your relationships. When you are fully present with someone, listening and engaging without distraction, you create genuine connection. People feel seen and valued when your attention is undivided. That is the kind of connection we all crave but rarely experience in a distracted world.

Over time, slowing down changes how you experience everything. You begin to find beauty in simplicity, satisfaction in small moments, and strength in softness. You learn that peace is not something to chase. It is something you allow.

The art of slowing down is ultimately the art of returning home to your body, your breath, and your life. It reminds you that you do not need to rush to be worthy. You only need to be present.

Chapter 5: Relearning Presence

Presence is one of the simplest things to understand yet one of the hardest to practice. It is the ability to be fully here, not just physically but mentally and emotionally. In a world that constantly pulls our attention elsewhere, being present has become a forgotten skill that we must now consciously relearn.

When was the last time you truly noticed what was around you? The way light falls through your window in the morning. The taste of your food when you are not multitasking. The tone in someone's voice when they speak to you. These small details are easy to miss when the mind is elsewhere, yet they are the essence of real living.

Presence is not about forcing yourself to focus. It is about gently returning to this moment again and again whenever your mind drifts away. It is a practice of awareness and acceptance. You notice your thoughts, your sensations, and your emotions without trying to change them.

So much of our attention is scattered. We are thinking about the past, worrying about the future, or mentally checking notifications even when our phones are silent. Our minds are often in many places at once, and presence brings us back to one.

Relearning presence begins by slowing your inner rhythm. Take a few deep breaths, feel your feet on the ground, and remind yourself that this moment is enough. You do not need to rush to the next thing. You do not need to capture it or prove it. Simply be in it.

One way to rebuild presence is through mindful observation. Pay attention to the small, quiet details that surround you. The sound of rain, the warmth of sunlight, the texture of your clothing, the rhythm of your own breath. When you notice them, you remind your body and mind that life is happening now.

Presence also means giving your full attention to the people you care about. When you listen deeply, without waiting to reply or thinking about what to say next, you create space for true connection. It is in those unguarded moments that relationships grow stronger.

Presence softens the edges of our daily stress. It turns ordinary moments into experiences of peace. It reminds us that we do not need more to feel fulfilled, we just need to fully experience what we already have.

Reflection Exercises:

- Spend five minutes today observing your surroundings without using your phone or other distractions. Notice colors, sounds, and sensations. Write down what stood out to you and how it made you feel.
- Choose one daily activity to turn into a mindful ritual such as eating breakfast, showering, or taking a walk. Focus completely on the experience itself. Feel each

movement, each breath, each sound. Let the ordinary become sacred.

Chapter 6: Nurturing Your Inner Garden

After learning to slow down and reclaim presence, the next step is nurturing your inner garden. Your mind and heart are like soil; they need care, attention, and the right environment to bloom. Without tending to them, distractions, stress, and old habits can take over, leaving little space for growth.

Nurturing your inner garden begins with awareness. Notice the thoughts, emotions, and routines that occupy your daily life. Which of them nourish you and which drain you? Just as a gardener observes the soil before planting, you must first understand your own inner landscape.

Self-care is the sunlight that allows your inner garden to thrive. It is not a luxury or an indulgence but a vital part of sustaining your energy and focus. Simple practices such as taking quiet moments for yourself, journaling, walking in nature, or practicing gentle meditation, act like sunlight, giving life and strength to your mental and emotional wellbeing.

Watering your inner garden means giving yourself consistent nourishment. This could be as simple as setting boundaries with your devices, choosing uplifting content, or dedicating time each day to activities that restore you. Small, steady acts of care accumulate over time and encourage your focus and calm to grow naturally.

Weeds, just like distractions, are inevitable. Old habits, anxious thoughts, or unnecessary digital noise can creep in if you are not attentive. The process of digital detox and emotional presence helps you notice these weeds early so you can gently remove them without harsh judgment. The goal is not perfection but balance, allowing space for your energy and creativity to flourish.

Blooming also involves planting seeds. These seeds can be new habits, creative projects, or moments of connection with yourself and others. Nurture them with patience and attention. Some seeds take longer to sprout than others. Some days your inner garden will feel full and vibrant, other days quiet and sparse. Both are natural and important stages of growth.

Reflection Exercises:

- Spend ten minutes imagining your inner garden. What does it look like? What is blooming? What needs more attention? Write down your thoughts and feelings. Visualizing your inner landscape helps clarify what aspects of your life require care and focus.
- Choose one small habit or practice to nurture yourself this week. It could be drinking water mindfully, taking a short walk without devices, or journaling each morning. Observe how this small act affects your energy and presence over time.

When you consistently nurture your inner garden, your energy, clarity, and creativity grow naturally. You begin to notice beauty in simple moments, joy in being present, and calm in the midst of life's noise. Blooming is not a destination. It is a journey, cultivated one intentional moment at a time.

Your inner garden reflects your attention and care. By giving it sunlight, water, and space to breathe, you reclaim your focus, reduce overwhelm, and create a sanctuary within yourself. In this quiet cultivation, you learn that growth is a gentle, ongoing process that allows you to bloom beyond the noise.

Chapter 7: Cultivating Mindful Habits

Reclaiming your focus and nurturing your inner garden is only the beginning. True transformation happens when you cultivate habits that support your presence, energy, and emotional wellbeing. Habits are the soil in which your growth flourishes, and mindful habits are the sunlight and water that ensure your inner garden blooms.

Mindful habits are small, intentional actions that bring awareness, calm, and purpose into your daily life. They can be as simple as taking three deep breaths before starting your day, pausing before checking your phone, or savoring a quiet cup of tea. Though small, these actions accumulate over time, creating a foundation for lasting presence and focus.

Start by observing your current routines. Which habits nurture your energy and which drain it? Awareness is the first step in change. Just as a gardener notices where weeds appear and where the soil is fertile, you must notice the rhythms of your own life to understand where growth is possible.

Once you are aware, gently introduce new habits that support your goals. Perhaps you start each morning with five minutes of mindful breathing, or you create a daily reflection journal to track your thoughts and emotions. The key is consistency, not intensity. Small, steady habits often produce the most lasting transformation.

Mindful habits also extend to your digital life. You can set boundaries for screen time, designate phone-free periods, or curate your feeds to show content that uplifts and inspires. These practices help protect your energy while allowing you to remain connected in ways that feel intentional rather than draining.

Reflection Exercise:

- Choose one daily habit that will help you reclaim your focus or energy. Commit to practicing it for one week and notice how it affects your mental clarity, mood, and presence. Write down any changes you observe.

Another important aspect of mindful habits is self-compassion. Growth is not linear, and some days will feel more challenging than others. Missing a habit or feeling distracted does not mean failure. It is simply part of the natural rhythm of cultivating change. Treat yourself with the same kindness and patience that you would offer a growing plant in your care.

Reflection Exercise:

- At the end of the day, write down one moment when you were fully present and one habit that supported that moment. Celebrate these small victories and use them to guide your next day.

Over time, these practices transform not only your routines but also your perspective. You begin to notice patterns of distraction, understand what truly nourishes you, and create space for growth. Mindful habits make room for your inner garden to thrive, allowing you to bloom with clarity, focus, and calm.

Blooming is not about doing everything perfectly. It is about creating a life that honors your energy, celebrates your moments of presence, and allows you to grow steadily. Your habits are the gentle hands that guide your attention, nurture your mind, and support your emotional wellbeing.

By cultivating mindful habits, you reclaim your focus, protect your energy, and prepare yourself for the deeper work of presence, creativity, and connection that follows. Every intentional choice you make, every small habit you nurture, is a step toward a life where you can truly bloom beyond the noise.

Chapter 8: Creative Recharge

Reclaiming your focus and nurturing mindful habits naturally leads to creativity. Your mind, once weighed down by constant notifications and digital clutter, now has the space to imagine, create, and explore. Creativity is not just for artists or writers. It is the energy to solve problems, see opportunities, and experience joy in everyday life.

A creative recharge is like sunlight for your inner garden. It invigorates, uplifts, and allows your mind to flourish. When you step away from screens and distractions, you give your imagination the freedom to grow. Even small actslike doodling, journaling, cooking mindfully, or walking in nature can spark insights and renew your energy.

Notice how your mind feels after a day of digital overload versus a day spent intentionally offline. Creativity thrives in quiet, reflective spaces where you are present and engaged. By cultivating these moments, you not only enhance your focus but also bring more vibrancy to your life.

Creative recharge begins with permission. Give yourself the freedom to explore without expectation or judgment. You do not need to produce a masterpiece or reach a goal. Simply allow yourself to play, experiment, and notice what arises. This is where true growth and inspiration emerge.

Reflection Exercise:

- Choose one activity this week that allows your mind to wander freely. It could be painting, writing, gardening, cooking, or walking in nature. Spend at least thirty minutes fully immersed and notice how your energy shifts.

Another way to recharge creatively is to step into curiosity. Observe the world around you — the patterns of leaves, the colors of a sunset, or the rhythm of city life. Ask questions, notice details, and let your mind make connections. Curiosity is a natural form of creativity that refreshes your perspective and opens new possibilities.

Even small pauses can spark creativity. A five-minute break from your phone, a quiet stretch, or mindful breathing can reset your brain and allow new ideas to surface. These tiny habits, when repeated, create an environment where your focus and imagination flourish together.

Reflection Exercise:

- Take a mindful break today. Step outside, notice your surroundings, and let your thoughts drift without pressure. Afterward, write down any new ideas, insights, or inspirations that arose.

Creative recharge is also about balance. It requires giving your mind rest, while also offering gentle stimulation that nurtures curiosity and engagement. Too much activity, even offline, can be draining. Too little can feel stagnant. Mindful attention to both rest and exploration creates a rhythm where your inner garden can thrive.

By consistently nurturing your creative energy, you allow yourself to bloom beyond distractions. Your focus deepens, your ideas grow clearer, and your experience of life becomes richer and more vibrant. Every intentional pause and mindful act contributes to your growth and presence.

Chapter 9: Intentional Connections

As your inner garden grows and your creative energy recharges, the next step is fostering intentional connections. Just as your mind and heart need nourishment, your relationships flourish when approached with presence, care, and purpose. In a world filled with constant notifications and superficial interactions, meaningful connection requires conscious effort.

Intentional connections are not measured by the number of friends, followers, or messages you exchange. They are defined by depth, authenticity, and mutual respect. These relationships allow you to share your energy, receive support, and grow together. They bloom in the space created by mindful attention and genuine presence.

Begin by observing your current connections. Which relationships uplift you, inspire you, or make you feel truly seen? Which ones drain your energy or feel shallow? Awareness is the first step in creating a circle of connection that nourishes rather than depletes.

Intentional connection also requires boundaries. Setting limits on digital communication, social media engagement, and time spent with others creates space for focus and calm. It allows you to show up fully when you are present, rather than fragmenting your attention across many distractions.

Reflection Exercise:

- Identify one relationship that you want to strengthen this week. Consider what actions you can take to be more present and supportive in this connection. Reach out, listen deeply, or spend quality time together without digital interruptions.

Another aspect of intentional connections is quality communication. Practice listening without planning your response, noticing nonverbal cues, and responding with empathy. Small acts of attentiveness create trust and deepen bonds.

Intentional connections are also about giving yourself grace. You cannot nurture every relationship perfectly, nor do you need to. Focus on the connections that matter most, where energy, presence, and mutual growth can flourish.

Reflection Exercise:

- Spend a mindful moment today appreciating one meaningful connection in your life. Reflect on how this relationship supports your growth and presence. Consider expressing gratitude to the person in a note, message, or in person.

As you cultivate intentional connections, notice how your own energy blooms. Presence and focus extend beyond yourself to the people around you. Just as a well-tended garden encourages growth in every plant, a mindful approach to relationships encourages connection, compassion, and joy.

Through intentional connections, you learn that true presence is not only internal but relational. The calm, clarity, and focus you've nurtured within yourself now radiate outward, creating a network of meaningful, supportive, and enriching interactions. This is the full expression of blooming beyond the noise.

Chapter 10: Bloom Beyond the Noise

You have journeyed through the distractions, the emotional clutter, and the constant pull of notifications. You have slowed down, reclaimed presence, nurtured your inner garden, cultivated mindful habits, and strengthened your creative energy. You have learned to connect intentionally and to care for yourself deeply. Now, it is time to bloom beyond the noise.

Blooming beyond the noise is not about perfection. It is about living intentionally, aligning your energy with your values, and choosing what deserves your attention. It is about listening to your inner voice, trusting your instincts, and honoring your need for calm, presence, and focus.

This bloom is both quiet and powerful. It does not announce itself with fanfare but grows steadily, nourished by the consistent care you have given your mind, heart, and soul. Each mindful choice, each moment of presence, each act of self-care adds water, sunlight, and love to your inner garden.

As you move forward, remember that the digital world will always be there. Notifications will still arrive, distractions will still tempt you, and the pace of life will continue to accelerate. The difference is that you now have tools to choose when to engage, when to pause, and when to protect your energy.

Your inner garden reflects your attention, your boundaries, and your care. By tending it regularly, you cultivate clarity, focus, and joy. You begin to notice what truly matters, to savor ordinary moments, and to celebrate the growth that happens quietly, steadily, and naturally.

Reflection Exercise:

- Take a moment to reflect on the journey you have taken through this book. What practices or lessons have had the most impact on your focus, calm, and presence? Which habits will you continue to nurture in your daily life?

Blooming beyond the noise is also about giving yourself permission to grow. Some days will be quieter, some days busier, and some moments may feel overwhelming. Accept each day as it comes, and return to your practices with patience and self-compassion. Growth is a journey, not a race.

Remember that blooming is a reflection of your attention, your choices, and your presence. Every pause, every mindful breath, every intentional act adds color, depth, and beauty to your life. You have the power to cultivate your inner garden and bloom, even in a world that never stops.

As you close this book, carry these lessons with you. Protect your focus, nurture your creativity, strengthen your connections, and continue to grow intentionally. Your bloom is unique, vibrant, and resilient. You have learned to thrive beyond the noise, and your life is ready to reflect the calm, clarity, and beauty that you have cultivated within yourself.

Bloom beyond the noise. Reclaim your focus. Live fully, gently, and intentionally.

Reflection Prompts

As you close this book, take a moment to turn inward.

These prompts are not questions to answer quickly. They are gentle invitations to pause and reflect. Write freely. Let your thoughts flow like petals opening toward light.

- When do I feel most peaceful, and what moments take that peace away?
- How does my body react when I spend too much time online?
- What kind of digital habits bring me joy, and which ones leave me feeling drained?
- Who or what am I truly seeking when I reach for my phone?
- How can I create space for silence in my daily routine?
- What does blooming beyond the noise mean to me personally?
- If I could design one mindful day without screens, how would it look and feel?
- What am I grateful for right now, in this quiet moment?

Take your time with these reflections. There is no rush. Your answers will shift and deepen as you grow.

7-Day Digital Detox Plan

A gentle seven-day reset to reconnect with peace, clarity, and balance. You don't need perfection, only intention.

Day 1

Silence all non-essential notifications. Notice the quiet.

Pay attention to how often your hand reaches for your phone out of habit.

Day 2

Unfollow, mute, or delete accounts that no longer align with your peace.

Curate your digital world like a garden. Only keep what nourishes.

Day 3

Have one meal, one walk, or one cup of tea without any devices.

Be fully present with the taste, sound, and feel of the moment.

Day 4

Spend time with someone in person. Let real laughter and conversation replace messages and emojis.

Day 5

Use your screen time to create something. Write, draw, cook, dance, or design.

Turn your energy inward and notice the difference it brings.

Day 6

Limit screen time two hours before bed. Read, stretch, or journal instead.

Sleep without your phone beside you and wake up with sunlight instead of scrolling.

Day 7

Spend the day without social media. Walk outside, talk to someone you love, or simply be with yourself.

Let stillness remind you of who you are beyond the noise.

Seeds of Stillness

Before you turn to your final reflection, take in these gentle reminders. Let them linger in your thoughts as you continue to bloom.

Presence is your most natural state.

Stillness is not empty; it is full of everything that matters.

The world slows down when you do.

Your peace is sacred, protect it gently.

Growth doesn’t have to be loud to be real.

Comparison steals joy, but gratitude restores it.

Every pause is a chance to begin again.

You are already becoming who you were meant to be.

Closing Reflection

You have made it through a journey of awareness, healing, and balance. Each page has invited you to slow down, reflect, and reconnect with the self that exists beneath the noise.

Remember, you are not required to be constantly available or endlessly productive to be worthy. You are allowed to rest. You are allowed to breathe. The world will wait while you nurture your peace.

As you continue beyond these pages, take with you the softness you've rediscovered — the joy of small moments, the beauty of stillness, and the courage to disconnect when needed.

Your bloom is quiet but powerful. You are living proof that peace can grow anywhere, even in the busiest corners of life.

Practical Exercises Recap

Throughout this book, you explored reflection exercises, mindful pauses, and creative recharges. Here is a quick reminder of some ways to continue your practice:

- Observe your surroundings for small, meaningful moments of presence.
- Journal daily reflections on thoughts, emotions, and intentions.
- Practice mindful breathing or meditation for a few minutes each day.
- Set boundaries for digital devices and notifications.
- Engage in activities that spark curiosity and creativity.
- Strengthen intentional relationships through presence and authentic communication.

These simple, consistent practices help maintain your focus, energy, and calm, allowing your inner garden to flourish continuously.

Gratitude

I am deeply grateful to my Mum and Dad, Mrs. Sumi Nagra and Mr. Navjot Singh Nagra, whose inspiration and encouragement planted the seed for this book. Their guidance, support, and belief in me reminded me to notice the small moments, nurture my inner self, and follow my passions.

Although I wrote this book as part of my hobby and personal interest, it reflects the lessons, values, and encouragement I have received from them.

To my readers, thank you for giving yourself the time, attention, and care to read this book. I hope it helps you cultivate a life that is calm, present, and full of growth.

From My Heart to Yours

Writing this book was never just about screens or silence. It was about finding balance in the modern world, learning to pause, and discovering the quiet spaces where we can reconnect with ourselves.

If these words reached you, even for a moment, if they offered comfort, inspiration, or simply made you pause, then it has done exactly what it was meant to do.

Every chapter, every reflection, and every gentle exercise was written with care, not as a prescription, but as an invitation. An invitation to notice your energy, your habits, your presence, and your capacity to bloom beyond the noise.

Thank you for giving yourself the time and attention to read these pages. Thank you for trusting yourself enough to explore small changes and quiet moments.

Your journey is ongoing. Each mindful choice, each pause, each intentional act of self-care is a seed planted in your life. Some days these seeds will grow quietly, almost imperceptibly. Other days, they will burst into vivid blooms of clarity, joy, and peace.

Keep blooming, gently, fully, and at your own pace. There is no rush. There is only your journey, and it is beautiful.

Gentle Reflection & Inspiration

Take a moment and notice your breath.

Notice the spaces between your thoughts.

Notice the small joys, the quiet moments, the gentle connections that fill your days.

This page is for stillness. Let yourself arrive fully in it. Let it remind you that balance doesn't come from deleting everything, but from learning to live consciously.

The calm you cultivate in your mind, in your heart, and in your digital habits is the same calm that allows your life to bloom.

Invitation to Bloom

Where in your life can you plant a seed of mindfulness today?

How can you protect your energy without guilt?

What small act of presence could you bring into your daily routine right now?

There is no wrong answer. There is only your choice to bloom, one mindful moment at a time.

Carry this awareness gently as you move forward. You are capable of more peace, clarity, and presence than you realize.

Connect and Continue Your Journey

Your journey does not end here. Keep nurturing your inner garden, reclaiming your focus, and blooming beyond the noise.

If you'd like to share your reflections or connect with others exploring mindful living, consider journaling your experiences, joining mindful communities, or simply observing and appreciating the growth happening in your life every day.